LE CORDON BLEU

HOME COLLECTION

·WINTER·

PERIPLUS
EDITIONS

# contents

*recipe ratings* ❂ *easy* ❂❂ *a little more care needed* ❂❂❂ *more care needed*

# Warm oyster mushroom salad

*Simple to prepare, this salad is nevertheless layered with texture and flavor. Warm, succulent oyster mushrooms nestle on a bed of crisp lettuce, doused with vinaigrette and sprinkled with celery root chips, to make an unusual starter or an excellent light luncheon dish.*

*Preparation time* **20 minutes**
*Total cooking time* **20 minutes**
*Serves 4–6*

**¹/2 celery root**
**a few drops of lemon juice**
**12 oz. oyster mushrooms**
**3–4 cups mixed salad leaves**
**1¹/2 tablespoons balsamic vinegar**
**¹/3 cup plus 1 tablespoon good-quality olive oil**
**oil, for deep-frying**
**4 shallots, chopped**

**1** Peel the celery root and cut into thin, even slices, placing them in a bowl of cold water with lemon juice added. Set aside until ready to use.

**2** Cut the mushrooms into large, bite-size pieces. Wash the salad leaves, then drain them and dry on paper towels or in a salad-spinner. Refrigerate to keep crisp.

**3** To make the vinaigrette, place the vinegar in a bowl with some salt and pepper and whisk together. Slowly add the ¹/3 cup oil in a steady stream, whisking constantly to form an emulsion. If the vinaigrette is too sharp, whisk in a little more oil.

**4** Preheat a deep-fat fryer or deep saucepan, one-third full of oil, to 375°F. Test the temperature by adding a single drained and dried celery root slice: if the oil bubbles vigorously around the chip, the oil is ready.

**5** Drain and dry the celery root slices thoroughly. Place a quarter of the celery root slices into a wire basket and lower the basket into the oil. Cook the slices for about 3 minutes, or until golden and crisp, stirring occasionally to encourage even coloring. Remove and drain on crumpled paper towels. Repeat in batches with the remaining slices. Sprinkle the drained chips with salt while they are still warm.

**6** Heat the 1 tablespoon olive oil in a deep skillet, add the shallots and cook gently, without coloring, until soft and transparent. Increase the heat to medium, add the mushrooms and toss quickly for 6–8 minutes.

**7** To assemble the salad, toss the salad leaves with the vinaigrette and arrange on serving plates. Spoon on the mushrooms and shallots mixture and sprinkle with celery root chips. Serve at once, while the mushrooms are still warm.

# Clear borscht with piroshki

*There are many variations of this popular Eastern European soup, yet the ingredient that always imparts its color is beets. This soup is very light and is served with piroshki: Russian potato and onion turnovers.*

*Preparation time 1 hour + 45 minutes standing*
*  + 1 hour refrigeration*
*Total cooking time 1 hour*
*Serves 4–6*

**PIROSHKI**
**1 cup all-purpose flour**
**1/4 oz. fresh yeast or 1/2 oz. dried yeast**
**  (2 tablespoons)**
**2 tablespoons warm milk**
**1 egg, beaten**
**3 tablespoons unsalted butter, at room temperature**
**2 small potatoes**
**1 small onion, finely diced**
**1 egg, beaten**
**oil, for deep-frying**

**BORSCHT**
**5 cups brown stock (see page 63)**
**2 large beets, about 9 oz. each, peeled**
**  and coarsely shredded**
**2 egg whites**
**1 tablespoon salt**
**1/2 teaspoon sugar**
**2 tablespoons lemon juice**
**snipped fresh chives, to garnish**

1  To make the piroshki dough, sift the flour and a pinch of salt into a bowl. Mix the yeast with the milk and stir until liquid. Pour the milk into the beaten egg, then add the mixture to the flour and mix together to a soft, sticky dough. Beat for 1 minute, or until smooth, then mix in 1 tablespoon of the butter until well combined. Cover with plastic wrap and leave in a warm place to rise for 30 minutes. Punch down the dough and chill for at least 1 hour, or overnight.

2  To make the piroshki filling, peel the potatoes and place in a large saucepan of salted water. Bring to a boil, then reduce the heat and simmer for 20–25 minutes, or until tender to the point of a knife. Drain the potatoes, cut into small cubes and set aside. Melt the remaining butter in a skillet, add the onion, then cover and cook gently for 5 minutes, or until soft. Increase the heat to medium, uncover the pan and cook for 2–3 minutes, or until a light golden brown. Remove from the heat, stir in the potato cubes and season well with salt and freshly ground pepper. Allow to cool.

3  To make the borscht, place the stock, beets, egg whites, salt, sugar, lemon juice and some finely ground black pepper in a large saucepan. Heat gently, whisking until a froth settles on top, then bring slowly to a boil. Remove from the heat and leave for 5 minutes.

4  Line a large strainer with cheesecloth and place over a clean pan. Strain the soup into the pan, discarding the contents of the cheesecloth. Season the soup to taste, adding more sugar or lemon juice for a sweet-and-sour flavor. Set aside.

5  On a well-floured surface, roll out the piroshki dough to an 1/8-inch thickness, then cut out 21/2-inch rounds using a plain cutter—you should have 8–12 rounds. Brush the edges of each round with a little beaten egg, and place a teaspoon of filling on one half of each. Fold the rounds over into turnovers, pinch the edges together to seal them, then leave the piroshki on a lightly floured tray for 10–15 minutes at room temperature.

6  Preheat a deep-fat fryer or deep saucepan, one-third full of oil, to 350°F. Cook the piroshki in batches until golden, then drain on crumpled paper towels and keep warm. Reheat the soup and transfer to warm serving bowls. Sprinkle the borscht with the snipped chives and serve the piroshki on the side.

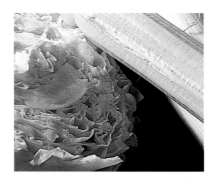

# Pot-au-feu

*Pot-au-feu literally means "pot on the fire," and the long, slow cooking of this classic dish will fill your kitchen with sumptuous aromas as it gently simmers to perfection. The traditional vegetables used in this recipe could be changed to suit the season or your personal taste.*

*Preparation time **30 minutes***
*Total cooking time **2 hours 45 minutes***
*Serves **6–8***

**2 small leeks**
**1 stalk celery or 1/2 small celery root**
**8–10 black peppercorns**
**5–6 coriander seeds**
**1/2 small green cabbage, cut into quarters**
**8 oz. oxtail, cut into small pieces**
**1 1/2 lb. beef ribs**
**1 small veal hock (see Chef's tips)**
**1 1/2 tablespoons salt**
**1 small onion, studded with 2 whole cloves**
**1 clove garlic**
**bouquet garni (see page 63)**
**2 carrots, cut into 2-inch pieces**
**1 turnip or rutabaga, peeled and quartered**

1  Tie the leeks and celery or celery root into a bundle. Place the peppercorns and coriander seeds in a small piece of cheesecloth, tie up and set aside. Place the cabbage in a large saucepan and cover with cold water.

Bring to a boil, cook for 3 minutes, then drain and rinse in cold water and set aside.

2  Rinse all the meat and bones, place them in a large pot and cover with cold water. Bring to a boil, then remove from the heat and drain. Rinse the meat again, return to the pot and cover with 3 1/2 quarts cold water. Add the salt and bring to a boil. Skim off the foam and any fat that rises to the surface. Add the onion, garlic, bouquet garni and the bag of peppercorns and coriander seeds. Simmer over low heat for at least 1 hour 45 minutes.

3  Add the carrots, turnip, cabbage and the leeks and celery bundle. Cook for another 30 minutes, or until the meat is tender. Remove and discard the bouquet garni and the bag of spices. Strain the meat and vegetables, reserving the broth. Arrange the meat on a large platter with the vegetables around, and serve the broth in a soup tureen.

***Chef's tips*** This dish is traditionally served with gherkins or sweet pickles, and salt for the meat.
  Boiled potatoes may be added to the broth.
  You can replace the veal hocks with ham or bacon bones but do not season the meat as it is already salty.

# Trout flans with chive and lemon sauce

*These delicately flavored and finely textured flans, served with a smooth lemon butter sauce, make an elegant first course to impress your friends and dinner guests.*

*Preparation time **30 minutes***
*Total cooking time **30 minutes***
*Serves 4*

**TROUT FLANS**
*fresh flat-leaf parsley leaves, to garnish*
*10 oz. skinned, trimmed and boned trout*
*1/4 teaspoon salt*
*pinch of cayenne pepper*
*I egg*
*2/3 cup heavy cream*
*3/4 cup milk*

**CHIVE AND LEMON SAUCE**
*I shallot, finely chopped*
*juice of I lemon*
*2/3 cup unsalted butter, chilled and cut into
  small cubes*
*I tablespoon very finely chopped fresh chives*

1  Preheat the oven to 325°F. Prepare four 3 x 1 1/2-inch individual soufflé dishes or custard cups by cutting four rounds of waxed paper to the same diameter. Grease the molds, then line them with the rounds of waxed paper and brush the lining with softened butter, pressing out any air holes. Press one or two parsley leaves onto the waxed paper, then set aside in the refrigerator.

2  To make the flan mixture, cut the trout into 1/2-inch cubes and place in a food processor with the salt, cayenne pepper and the egg. Blend until smooth. Scrape

down with a spatula and process again. With the machine still running, add the cream and milk, stopping the moment the liquid is incorporated—the mixture should resemble a cake batter. Push the mixture through a strainer into a pitcher.

3  Pour the mixture into the molds, tapping them on a work surface to remove any air bubbles. Smooth the tops and transfer the molds to a small roasting pan lined with one or two sheets of paper towel, spacing them evenly apart. Fill the pan with boiling water to come halfway up the sides of the molds; transfer to the oven and bake for 15–20 minutes. Insert a small knife in the center of a mold for 3 seconds. If the blade comes out hot, the flans are cooked. Remove from the hot water bath and set aside to rest. Keep warm.

4  To make the chive and lemon sauce, place the shallot and lemon juice in a small saucepan. Add 2 tablespoons water, bring to a boil and allow to reduce for about 5–7 minutes, or until almost dry. Reduce the heat to low, then whisk in the butter, a few pieces at a time, without letting the sauce boil. Strain into a clean pan and season to taste with salt and freshly ground white pepper. Just before serving, whisk in the chives.

5  Loosen the flans from the inside of the molds using a small knife. Gently turn the flans out onto individual serving plates. Carefully remove the paper, drizzle the sauce around and serve immediately.

*Chef's tip* When making a lightly colored sauce, use ground white pepper rather than black pepper as the white pepper will not show.

# Scallops dieppoise

*Dieppe, on the northern coast of France, is renowned for seafood specialties such as this. "Dieppoise" dishes usually contain shrimp, mussels, mushrooms and white wine.*

Preparation time **1 hour**
Total cooking time **50 minutes**
**Serves 4**

I large shallot, chopped
1 1/2 cups white wine
2 sprigs of fresh thyme
I bay leaf
8 oz. fresh mussels, scrubbed and beards removed
8 oz. small uncooked shrimp, peeled and deveined
20 fresh or frozen scallops, patted dry
3 cups sliced button mushrooms
3/4 cup heavy cream
I tablespoon chopped fresh flat-leaf parsley

1 Place the shallot, wine, thyme, bay leaf and mussels in a large pot. Bring to a boil, reduce the heat and simmer, covered, until the mussels open, tossing gently once or twice. Remove the mussels and allow to cool, discarding any that have not opened.

2 Line a fine strainer with damp cheesecloth and strain the liquid into a large saucepan. Discard the contents of the cheesecloth, rinse it well, and set it up as before.

3 Bring the liquid to a simmer. Add the shrimp, stir, then add the scallops. Cover and simmer for 5 minutes, or until the seafood is firm. Remove the seafood and set aside. Scoop the mussels from their shells and set aside.

4 Strain the cooking liquid through the cheesecloth into a saucepan. Bring to a boil, add the mushrooms and cook for about 25 minutes, or until almost dry. Add the cream and boil for 5 minutes. Add the seafood and simmer until hot. Season to taste and stir in the parsley just before serving.

# Consommé with chicken quenelles

*A consommé is a clarified meat or fish broth that should be crystal-clear and full of flavor.
Here it is served with light chicken quenelles and garnished with chervil.*

*Preparation time* **30 minutes + chilling**
*Total cooking time* **2 hours 40 minutes**
*Serves 4–6*

**I chicken, about 3¹/₂ lb.**
**I chicken leg and thigh quarter**
**2–3 sets of giblets, minus the liver (optional)**
**I large carrot**
**I large onion, studded with a whole clove**
**I stalk celery**
**I leek**
**I ripe tomato**
**sprig of fresh thyme**
**5 fresh parsley stalks**
**I bay leaf**
**6 black peppercorns**
**2 cloves garlic, crushed**
**2 teaspoons brandy**
**sprigs of fresh chervil, to garnish**

**QUENELLES**
**I egg white**
**¹/₄ cup plus I tablespoon heavy cream**
**small pinch of freshly grated nutmeg**

**FOR THE CLARIFICATION**
**I small carrot, chopped**
**¹/₂ stalk celery, chopped**
**¹/₂ leek, chopped**
**I tomato, chopped**
**3 egg whites, lightly beaten**

1  Remove the breast meat from the chicken, discarding the skin. Reserve and refrigerate for the quenelles. Bone the chicken leg and thigh, discarding all the skin and fat. Chop the meat, cover and refrigerate for the clarification of the stock.

2  Place the remaining chicken meat and bones in a large saucepan with the giblets. Add enough cold water to cover and bring to a boil. Drain, rinse with cold water and return to the pan.

3  Add the whole vegetables, thyme, parsley, bay leaf, peppercorns and garlic, with 3¹/₂ quarts water and some salt. Bring to a boil, reduce the heat and simmer gently for 1¹/₂–2 hours, skimming occasionally. Leave to cool, then remove the chicken and set aside. Strain the stock (there should be about 1¹/₂ quarts) into a clean pan, discarding the solids. Refrigerate, then skim off any fat.

4  To make the quenelles, purée the chicken breast in a food processor. Add the egg white, and process until smooth and superfine. Transfer to a bowl placed in another bowl of iced water, then gradually beat in the cream. Season with salt, pepper and nutmeg.

5  Bring the stock to a simmer in a large saucepan. Test the chicken breast mixture for seasoning and shape into quenelles, following the Chef's techniques on page 62. Poach the quenelles in the simmering stock in batches for 5 minutes, or until just firm enough to remove with a slotted spoon. Place on a serving plate, cover and set aside.

6  Slightly overseason the stock. To clarify the stock, add the chicken leg meat, chopped carrot, celery, leek, tomato and egg whites. Mix well. Slowly bring to a boil, stirring until the egg whites solidify into a soft foamy crust. Reduce the heat to low and allow to simmer for 20–25 minutes.

7  Without pressing the solids, carefully strain the stock through a cheesecloth-lined strainer into a clean saucepan; discard the solids. Reheat the consommé and add the brandy. Place the quenelles in bowls, ladle the consommé over and garnish with the chervil.

# Country-style terrine

*This coarsely textured pâté derives its name from the deep rectangular dish in which it is cooked. Meat terrines often contain a high proportion of pork, and some pork fat, to prevent the meat from becoming dry.*

*Preparation time **30 minutes + 2 nights refrigeration***
*Total cooking time **50 minutes***
***Serves 6–8***

**1 1/2 tablespoons unsalted butter**
**2 cloves garlic, chopped**
**2 shallots, chopped**
**3 sprigs of fresh thyme**
**1 small bay leaf**
**6 oz. pork fat, finely diced**
**5 oz. calf, lamb or ox liver, finely diced**
**12 oz. pork tenderloin, finely diced**
**3 tablespoons brandy**
**3 tablespoons white wine**
**1/2 teaspoon salt**
**1/4 teaspoon ground nutmeg**
**2/3 cup fresh bread crumbs**
**1 tablespoon milk**
**1 egg, beaten**
**20 slices bacon, for lining**

1 Melt the butter in a deep skillet over low heat. Warm the garlic, shallots, thyme and bay leaf with the pork fat, liver and diced pork. Gently cook for 3–5 minutes. Add the brandy, wine, salt, nutmeg and some pepper, stirring well to coat the meat—the mixture should be warm, not hot. Allow to cool, then refrigerate overnight.

2 Preheat the oven to 350°F. Wrap a small piece of wood or stiff cardboard (the same size as the top of a 1-quart terrine) in aluminum foil. Soak the bread crumbs in milk.

3 Remove the thyme and bay leaf from the terrine mixture. Process the meat in a food processor in short bursts until coarsely chopped, then transfer to a bowl. Mix together the bread crumbs and egg and add to the meat. Mix well.

4 Line a greased terrine mold with bacon, letting the slices hang over the sides. Add the meat mixture, fold the slices over and cover with a layer of bacon, then a sheet of greased waxed paper. Place in a baking pan half-filled with hot water and bake for 30–40 minutes. To check the temperature, insert the tip of a small knife into the center of the terrine for a few seconds. If the blade comes out hot, the terrine is cooked; if not, cook for another 5 minutes, or until the knife comes out hot.

5 Remove from the oven and cool for 20 minutes. Place the wood or cardboard across the top, then weight it down with a heavy can. Refrigerate overnight. Leave the terrine at room temperature for at least 30 minutes before serving. It can be served in the mold, or turned out onto a board or plate.

# Beef Wellington

*Beef Wellington is the name given to loin of beef, lightly covered with duxelles (shallots and mushrooms cooked in butter) and/or a good liver pâté, then wrapped in puff pastry and baked until golden.*

*Preparation time **1 hour + 15 minutes chilling***
*Total cooking time **1 hour 15 minutes***
*Serves 6*

3¹/4 lb. beef rib-eye roast
¹/2 cup oil
I small carrot, chopped
I small onion, chopped
I small leek, chopped
3 tablespoons dry Madeira or sherry
2 cups brown stock (see page 63)
3 tablespoons unsalted butter
2 shallots, finely chopped
I clove garlic, finely chopped
I lb. button mushrooms, finely chopped
2–3 sheets frozen puff pastry, thawed
10 slices prosciutto
I egg, beaten

1  Preheat the oven to 425°F. Remove and reserve the thin muscle from the side of the beef. Remove and discard the shiny surface membrane and tie the meat with string at 3/4-inch intervals.

2  Coarsely chop the beef trimmings. Heat 1 tablespoon of the oil in a skillet, then add the beef trimmings and chopped carrot, onion and leek. Gently fry until the mixture browns. Stir in the Madeira, scraping up the sticky juices from the base of the pan, then simmer for a few minutes, or until reduced to a syrup. Stir in the stock. Bring to a boil, then reduce the heat and leave for 1 hour to simmer to a syrupy sauce while preparing the Beef Wellington.

3  Place a roasting pan over high heat and add the remaining oil. When a haze forms, add the beef roast and brown quickly all over. Season well, then transfer to the oven and roast for about 5 minutes for medium rare, 10 minutes for medium and 15 minutes for well done. (The actual roasting time will depend on the thickness of the beef.) Remove from the pan to cool completely.

4  Melt the butter in a saucepan and gently cook the shallots for 1–2 minutes, or until soft but not browned. Add the garlic and mushrooms and cook gently until the pan looks dry when scraped with a wooden spoon. The mixture should be barely moist. Set aside.

5  On a lightly floured work surface, slightly overlap the pastry sheets and roll out into a rectangle 24 x 14 inches. Transfer to a baking sheet, cover with plastic wrap and refrigerate for 15 minutes.

6  Transfer the pastry to the work surface. To reduce excess overlap, cut away each corner, reserving the pastry trimmings and leaving the center large enough for the beef—the pastry will resemble a cross. Flatten each flap of pastry with a rolling pin.

7  Lay the prosciutto slices on the pastry and spread thinly with half the mushrooms. Untie the beef, season well, place it on the pastry and spread with the remaining mushrooms. Bring the flaps of prosciutto over the beef. Brush the pastry edges with a little beaten egg and fold them over each other to completely encase the beef.

8  Turn onto a lightly buttered baking sheet, seam-side-down. Cut the excess pastry into strips and crisscross a lattice pattern over the top. Brush with more beaten egg, then pierce a small slit in the top for a crisp finish. Place in the oven for 5 minutes to set, then lower the heat to 400°F and bake for 20 minutes.

9  Remove from the oven and allow to rest for 10 minutes in a warm place. Skim any froth from the simmering sauce, then strain into a gravy boat. Slice the Beef Wellington and serve at once with the gravy served alongside.

# Lamb medallions with red currant sauce

*This superb dish, with its classic combination of red currant and lamb, may seem very time consuming.
Rest assured, it isn't: Most of the cooking time revolves around a gently simmering pot.*

*Preparation time **45 minutes + overnight marinating***
*Total cooking time **2 hours 10 minutes***
**Serves 4**

**3 x 7-rib racks of lamb (ask your butcher to debone
the lamb, remove the fat, chop the bones and
reserve the trimmings)**
**oil, for cooking**
**I tablespoon tomato paste**
**I tablespoon sugar**
**I tablespoon red wine vinegar**
**I teaspoon crushed black pepper**
**2 tablespoons red currant jelly**
**I cup brown stock
(see page 63)**

**MARINADE**
**I carrot, diced**
**I onion, diced**
**I stalk celery, diced**
**I shallot, diced**
**2 tomatoes, diced**
**4 juniper berries**
**4 cloves garlic, split in half**
**I tablespoon red wine vinegar**
**I tablespoon oil**
**bouquet garni (see page 63)**
**6 cups full-bodied red wine
(such as Cabernet Sauvignon)**

**1** Place the lamb bones and trimmings in a large bowl
with all the marinade ingredients except the wine. Bring
the wine to a boil in a saucepan, then pour directly into
the marinade bowl. Leave to cool, then add the lamb
and marinate overnight, or for a maximum of 48 hours.

**2** Remove the lamb portions from the marinade. Pat
dry, cover with plastic wrap and refrigerate until ready
to use. Strain the marinade into a pan, reserving the
bones and vegetables. Bring to a boil, then reduce
the heat and leave to simmer gently while browning
the bones.

**3** Heat about 2 tablespoons of oil in a large saucepan.
Brown the bones over medium heat for 10–15 minutes,
or until dry and well colored, stirring constantly to
prevent burning. Drain the saucepan of excess oil and
return the bones to the saucepan. Add the vegetables
and cook for 2–3 minutes, or until lightly colored. Mix
in the tomato paste and cook for 1 minute.

**4** Strain the hot marinade into the saucepan and bring
to a boil, scraping the base of the saucepan to dissolve
the cooking juices. Add enough water to cover the bones
completely, then reduce the heat and simmer for
1 hour, skimming regularly. Strain the sauce through a
fine sieve and discard the bones and vegetables. Cook
for about 20 minutes, or until reduced in volume to
1 cup, skimming regularly.

**5** In a heavy-bottomed saucepan, melt the sugar over
medium heat for 2–3 minutes, or until caramelized.
Remove from the heat and immediately add the vinegar,
taking care not to breathe in the fumes. Mix until the
caramel dissolves, then add the pepper, half the red
currant jelly, the stock and reduced marinade. Simmer
for 5 minutes, then strain through a fine sieve, into a
clean saucepan. Cook for another 5 minutes, or until the
sauce is thick enough to coat the back of a spoon. Stir in
the rest of the red currant jelly. Season with salt and
keep warm.

**6** Cut the lamb into 16 medallions, each about 1 inch
thick. Heat 2 tablespoons of oil in a skillet over medium
heat. Season the medallions with salt and pepper, then
cook for 2–3 minutes on each side. Serve with the sauce.

# Pork chops with sage

*Sage, a wonderfully redolent herb, marries perfectly with the tang of mustard in this delectable dish.*

*Preparation time* **15 minutes**
*Total cooking time* **45 minutes**
*Serves 4*

**4 pork chops cut from the rib, about 6 oz. each**
**8 fresh sage leaves**
**2 tablespoons unsalted butter**
**oil, for cooking**
**2 shallots, finely chopped**
**2 teaspoons light-colored honey**
**juice of 1/2 lemon**
**3/4 cup white wine**
**1 1/2 cups brown stock (see page 63)**
**2 tablespoons Dijon mustard**

**1** Preheat the oven to 350°F. Trim the pork chops well and season with salt and pepper. Set aside the four nicest sage leaves to garnish, and finely shred the others.
**2** Heat the butter and a tablespoon of oil in an ovenproof skillet. Brown the chops on both sides over medium heat, then transfer to the oven and roast for 15 minutes.
**3** Once cooked, remove the chops from the pan; cover and keep warm. Add the shallots to the pan and cook over medium heat, without coloring, for 2–3 minutes, then add the honey and lemon juice and cook until the mixture is syrupy.
**4** Add the wine, scraping the bottom of the pan well. Add the stock and simmer for 10–15 minutes, or until reduced in volume by half. Whisk in the mustard, being careful not to let the sauce boil.
**5** Strain the sauce, mix in the shredded sage, and adjust the seasoning. Coat the warm chops with the sauce, garnish each with a sage leaf and serve immediately.

# Roast duck with turnips

*Roasting a duck on each side before turning it onto its back will make sure the meat does not dry out. The salty bacon and sweetened turnips perfectly complement this succulent dish.*

*Preparation time* **40 minutes**
*Total cooking time* **1 hour 40 minutes**
*Serves 4*

2³/4 lb. duck, trussed (ask your butcher
   to do this)
oil, for cooking
1/4 cup unsalted butter, softened
6 oz. duck trimmings (wings or necks),
   chopped
6 large turnips
10 oz. lean bacon, cut into
   1/2-inch cubes
1 tablespoon unsalted butter
1 teaspoon sugar
1 shallot, chopped
1 tablespoon chopped celery
1 tablespoon chopped carrot
1 tablespoon chopped onion
3 cups chicken stock (see page 62)
bouquet garni (see page 63)

1  Preheat the oven to 400°F. Coat a roasting pan with 2 tablespoons of oil. Season the duck, rub it all over with oil and place it on its side in the pan. Dot with the softened butter, transfer to the oven and roast for 20 minutes, basting every 5 minutes. Turn the duck onto its other side and roast for 20 more minutes, basting as

before. Turn the duck on its back, add the duck trimmings, then roast and baste for another 15 minutes.

2  Peel the turnips and use a melon-baller to scoop the flesh into little balls. Place the balls in cold water until ready to use.

3  In a skillet, heat some oil and brown the bacon over medium heat. Strain and set aside. Drain and dry the turnips; place in the pan with the butter, sugar and some salt. Cover with cold water and cook over high heat until evaporated. Roll the turnips until coated and shiny. Remove from the heat, add the bacon and set aside.

4  Remove the duck from the roasting pan; cover and keep warm. Remove and drain the trimmings. Drain the pan of all but 2 tablespoons of the oil and duck juices and place over low heat for 10 minutes, or until the juices are sticky and the fat is clear.

5  Add the trimmings and chopped vegetables and cook for 2 minutes. Add the stock and bouquet garni; stir well and pour into a saucepan. Bring to a boil, reduce the heat and simmer, skimming occasionally, for 20–30 minutes, or until the sauce is reduced by half. Strain, discarding the solids; season and keep warm.

6  Remove the string and place the duck on a platter. Reheat the bacon and turnips and arrange around the duck. Drizzle half the sauce over the bacon and turnips and serve the remaining sauce on the side.

*Chef's tip* For instructions on carving the duck, refer to the Chef's techniques on page 63.

# Blanquette of lamb in garlic cream

*Blanquette de veau, a very traditional French stew, has here been updated into a modern classic, using lamb in place of the veal and flavored heartily with garlic.*

*Preparation time* **20 minutes**
*Total cooking time* **1 hour 40 minutes**
*Serves 6*

**3 lb. boneless lamb shoulder**
**1 carrot**
**1 small onion**
**1 stalk celery**
**1 sprig of fresh thyme or**
  **¹/2 teaspoon dried thyme**
**bay leaf**
**1 teaspoon salt**
**10–12 peppercorns**
**8 unpeeled cloves garlic**
**¹/3 cup olive oil**
**2 tablespoons unsalted butter**
**¹/4 cup all-purpose flour**
**1¹/4 cups whipping cream**
**finely chopped fresh parsley, to garnish**

1  Trim the lamb of excess fat and cut the meat into 1¹/4-inch cubes. Place the lamb cubes in a large flameproof casserole or Dutch oven with the whole carrot, onion, celery stalk, the thyme, bay leaf, salt and peppercorns. Add cold water to reach 1 inch above the meat and vegetables. Bring to a boil, then reduce the heat and simmer for about 1 hour 10 minutes, skimming any froth from the surface.

2  Meanwhile, set the oven to its lowest temperature. Place the garlic cloves in a small baking dish and cover with the olive oil. Cook for 40 minutes, or until soft. Drain and peel the garlic cloves, then press through a sieve to obtain a purée.

3  Strain the lamb and reserve the liquid. Discard the vegetables and keep the lamb warm. Return the liquid to the casserole and simmer over low heat for 20 minutes, or until reduced by half, skimming off the excess fat.

4  Melt the butter in a saucepan over low heat. Add the flour and cook for 1 minute. Add the reduced cooking liquid and whisk to a boil. Add the cream and mix until smooth, then add the garlic purée. Strain the sauce and season to taste with salt and freshly ground pepper. Arrange the lamb in a deep serving dish and cover with the sauce. Sprinkle with the parsley and serve at once.

# Roast beef and Yorkshire puddings

*What could be more tantalizing or traditionally British than roast beef served with crisp, golden Yorkshire puddings and tangy horseradish cream? Carve the beef at the table for the greatest effect.*

*Preparation time 40 minutes + 30 minutes resting*
*Total cooking time 1 hour 40 minutes*
*Serves 4–6*

**YORKSHIRE PUDDINGS**
*3/4 cup milk*
*1 1/2 cups all-purpose flour*
*2 eggs*

*oil, for cooking*
*3 lb. boneless beef roast (round tip or rib)*

**HORSERADISH CREAM**
*1/2 cup whipping cream*
*2–3 tablespoons grated fresh or bottled white horseradish*
*a few drops of lemon juice*

**JUS**
*1 carrot, chopped*
*1 onion, chopped*
*1 stalk celery, chopped*
*1 leek, chopped*
*1 bay leaf*
*2 sprigs of fresh thyme*
*3 peppercorns*
*2 cups brown stock (see page 63)*

1  Preheat the oven to 425°F. To make the Yorkshire puddings, combine the milk with 1/2 cup water. Sift the flour and some salt into a bowl and make a well in the center. Add the eggs and begin to whisk. As the mixture thickens, gradually add the milk and water, whisking until a smooth batter forms. Pour into a pitcher, cover and stand for 30 minutes.

2  On the stove top, heat about 1/4 cup of oil in a roasting pan over high heat. Add the beef, fat-side-down, and brown all over, turning with tongs. Transfer the beef to the oven and, turning and basting every 15 minutes, roast for 30 minutes for rare, 45 minutes for medium-rare, and 1 hour for well done.

3  To make the horseradish cream, lightly whip the cream until soft peaks form. Gently fold in the horseradish and season to taste with salt, pepper and the lemon juice. Do not overfold or the mixture will become too thick. Transfer to a serving bowl, cover and chill.

4  Transfer the beef to a plate, cover lightly with foil and allow to rest for 10–15 minutes before carving. Leaving a tablespoon of fat in the roasting pan, drain the excess fat and use it to brush a deep, 12-hole muffin pan.

5  Heat the muffin pan in the oven for 2–3 minutes until lightly smoking. Divide the Yorkshire pudding batter between the cups and bake for 15–20 minutes, or until puffed and golden.

6  To make the jus, heat the remaining fat in the roasting pan over the stove top. Add the vegetables and gently fry over medium heat for 5 minutes, or until golden, stirring constantly. Drain the pan of any excess fat; add the bay leaf, thyme, peppercorns and a little hot stock, scraping the base of the pan with a wooden spoon. Add the remaining hot stock and simmer to reduce by half, skimming off any foam or fat. Strain into a saucepan, discarding the vegetables and seasonings. Skim again, season to taste, then cover and keep warm. (Pour into a warm gravy boat just before serving.)

7  Serve the beef and puddings on warm plates, with the jus and horseradish cream on the side. Green vegetables and roast potatoes are traditional accompaniments.

*Chef's tip* Resting a roast makes the meat easier to carve and helps prevent the juices running. Any juices from the resting can be poured over the meat, but do not add them to the jus: they will spoil its texture.

# Salmon, leek and potato gratin

*This wonderful recipe, combining fresh and smoked salmon, is perfect for a special lunch or supper. A more economical version, also delicious, could be made using any fresh fish, or even salt cod.*

*Preparation time **20 minutes***
*Total cooking time **50 minutes***
*Serves 6*

**1³/4 lb. potatoes**
**³/4 cup unsalted butter, softened**
**3 small leeks, thinly sliced**
**5 oz. fresh salmon fillet, skinned**
**6 oz. smoked salmon, diced**
**1¹/4 cups whipping cream**
**³/4 cup shredded Swiss cheese**
**3 tablespoons unsalted butter, chopped**
**sprigs of fresh dill, to garnish**

**1** Peel the potatoes and place in a large saucepan of salted water. Bring to a boil, then reduce the heat and simmer for 20–25 minutes, or until tender to the point of a knife. Drain and finely mash the potatoes, or purée them using a food mill or ricer. Mix in half the softened butter and keep warm.

**2** Melt the remaining softened butter in a skillet over low heat. Gently cook the leeks for 2–3 minutes, without coloring. Drain the excess butter and spread the leeks evenly in an oval gratin dish. Set aside.

**3** Remove any fine bones from the fresh salmon using a pair of tweezers. Place the fillet in a steamer basket, then cover and steam for 5–10 minutes, or until the fish changes color and begins to break apart when pressed with a fork. Break the fish into pieces and mix into the mashed potato with the smoked salmon.

**4** Preheat the broiler to hot. Bring the cream to a boil in a small saucepan, then stir into the salmon and potato mixture. Mix well and season to taste. Transfer to the gratin dish and sprinkle with the shredded cheese. Dot with the butter and brown under the broiler for 2–3 minutes, or until golden. Serve garnished with sprigs of dill.

***Chef's tip*** To use salt cod in this recipe, rinse and soak it overnight, then poach in milk with a few sprigs of fresh thyme, a bay leaf and a few garlic cloves until tender. Drain, break into small pieces, then add to the potato mixture.

You can also use smoked haddock for this recipe, but there is no need to soak it overnight before poaching.

# Normandy pork

*Normandy lies along France's northern Atlantic coastline and is famous for its dairy farming and apple production. Not surprisingly, the cuisine of this region often features apples, cream, cider or Calvados—or sometimes all four, as in this superb dish.*

*Preparation time* **25 minutes**
*Total cooking time* **55 minutes**
*Serves 4*

**2 small apples, such as Golden Delicious**
**juice of 1/2 lemon**
**1/3 cup unsalted butter**
**1 1/4 lb. pork tenderloin**
**oil, for cooking**
**1 onion, chopped**
**1 carrot, chopped**
**sprig of fresh thyme**
**1 bay leaf**
**1 1/2 cups hard cider**
**1 tablespoon Calvados or applejack**
**1 1/2 cups heavy cream**

**1** Peel and core the apples, reserving the cores and peelings. Cut the apples into 1/2-inch cubes (keep all the trimmings) and toss them in the lemon juice. In a non-stick skillet, melt half the butter and cook the apples over medium heat for 5 minutes, or until golden brown.

Drain and transfer to a plate, spreading out the apples to help them cool quickly.

**2** Trim the fat and sinew from the pork, reserving the trimmings. Cut the pork into thick medallions and season well.

**3** Heat the remaining butter and a tablespoon of oil in a heavy-bottomed skillet. Cook the pork medallions over medium heat for 8 minutes on each side, or until nicely colored. Remove from the pan, cover with aluminum foil, set aside and keep warm.

**4** Add the pork trimmings to the pan and brown for 5–7 minutes, or until golden. Drain the pan of excess oil, then add the apple trimmings, onion, carrot, thyme and bay leaf. Cook over medium heat for 5–7 minutes.

**5** Add the cider and Calvados and cook for 5 minutes, or until reduced in volume by half. Add the cream, reduce the heat and simmer for 10 minutes. Strain the sauce, discard the solids and simmer for 1 minute more before adding the diced cooked apple. Cook for another 2 minutes, then season to taste. Keep hot.

**6** Transfer the pork medallions to a skillet. Pour the sauce over them and simmer for 2–3 minutes, or until heated through.

# Roast lamb with vegetables

*This memorable roast is served with a classic French garnish of bacon, mushrooms, glazed onions and golden brown potatoes. It makes a special dish for a Sunday lunch with all the family.*

*Preparation time* **1 hour 15 minutes**
*Total cooking time* **1 hour**
*Serves 6*

**1/3 cup oil**
**1 boneless lamb shoulder roast, about 3 lb.**
**(ask your butcher to reserve some of the bones and trimmings)**
**1 carrot, chopped**
**1 onion, chopped**
**1/2 stalk celery, chopped**
**2 cloves garlic, crushed**
**1 sprig of fresh thyme or 1/4 teaspoon dried thyme**
**1 bay leaf**
**10 oz. bacon**
**12 tiny boiling onions, peeled**
**1/3 cup unsalted butter**
**1 tablespoon sugar**
**24 button mushrooms**
**4 potatoes, peeled**
**1 1/2 cups chicken stock**
**(see page 62)**
**2 tablespoons chopped fresh parsley**

1  Preheat the oven to 400°F. Heat half the oil in a roasting pan over high heat. Season the lamb and brown on all sides in the hot oil. Remove and set aside. Add the bones and trimmings to the pan and brown all over.

2  Add the carrot, onion, celery, garlic, thyme and bay leaf to the pan. Rest the lamb on the bones, then transfer to the oven and roast for 40 minutes for rare, or 1 hour for medium, basting two or three times.

3  Cut the bacon into 1/8-inch pieces. In a skillet, lightly brown the bacon, then drain. Place the onions in a medium saucepan over high heat with 1 tablespoon of the butter, the sugar, 3 tablespoons water, and salt and freshly ground pepper to taste. Cook until the water has evaporated and the onions are a light blond color.

4  Cut the mushrooms into quarters, then sauté them in 2 tablespoons of the butter over high heat until browned. Season to taste and drain.

5  Using a melon-baller, carve the potatoes into balls, placing them in cold water to prevent browning, then transfer to a pan of cold water. Bring to a boil, boil for 1 minute, then drain.

6  Heat the remaining oil in an ovenproof skillet over high heat. When the oil is hot, add the potatoes, tossing to coat them evenly with oil. Cook for 2–3 minutes, or until well colored, then transfer to the oven and bake for 20 minutes, or until tender. Drain off the excess oil, toss the potato balls in the remaining butter and season to taste with salt and freshly ground black pepper.

7  Remove the lamb from the oven and place on a wire rack to rest. Drain the pan of excess fat, remove the bones and trimmings, and place the pan on the stove top over medium-high heat. Cook for 2–3 minutes, or until the vegetables have colored, then add the stock and stir to dissolve the cooking juices. Cook for about 10 minutes, or until reduced in volume by a third. Strain and season to taste with salt and pepper.

8  Toss together the onions, potatoes, mushrooms and bacon and reheat if necessary. Sprinkle with the chopped parsley. Carve the lamb into slices about 1/2-inch thick; serve surrounded with the vegetables and bacon, and the sauce on the side.

# Steak and kidney pudding

*Originally from Sussex, this famous English dish features morsels of steak and kidney in a thick, rich gravy, enclosed in suet pastry. It can be enriched with the addition of mushrooms, or even oysters.*

*Preparation time **50 minutes***
*Total cooking time **4 hours***
***Serves 6***

**3 tablespoons all-purpose flour**
**I lb. chuck steak, cut into 1/2-inch cubes**
**6 oz. ox or calf kidney, core removed,**
   **cut into 1/4-inch pieces**
**6–8 button mushrooms, quartered**
**2 small onions, finely chopped**
**2 tablespoons chopped fresh parsley**
**I tablespoon Worcestershire sauce**
**1/4–1/2 cup brown stock (see page 63)**

**SUET PASTRY**
**2 3/4 cups self-rising flour**
**6 oz. beef suet, grated**

**1** Grease a 1 1/2-quart pudding mold. Place the flour in a large bowl, season with salt and pepper, then toss with the steak and kidney. Add the mushrooms, onions, parsley and Worcestershire sauce. Mix lightly, season, and set aside. Place an upturned saucer or trivet in a large wide pot, fill to a third with water and bring to a boil.

**2** To make the suet pastry, sift the flour and some salt into a bowl. Toss in the suet and make a well in the center. Mix lightly using a round-bladed knife, then gradually add just enough water to obtain a reasonably stiff paste.

**3** On a well-floured surface, roll out two-thirds of the pastry to fit the mold. Carefully ease the pastry into the mold, checking there are no creases, and extending the pastry over the edges of the mold. Roll out the remaining pastry to a circle 5/8 inch thick and the same size as the top of the pudding mold. Set aside as a lid. Fill the pastry-lined mold with the meat, adding enough stock to cover the meat. Turn the excess pastry over the filling and moisten lightly, then press the pastry lid on lightly to seal.

**4** Cover with waxed paper, then aluminum foil, turning the edges under. Cover with a dish towel and tie some kitchen string securely under the rim to keep it in place. As a handle, tie a knot over the pudding with the cloth ends. Place on the saucer in the pan of simmering water, cover the pot and steam for 4 hours, adding boiling water as needed so the pan does not boil dry.

**5** Remove the cloth, foil and paper and clean the outside of the mold. Wrap a clean napkin around and serve the pudding from the mold, or turn the pudding out onto a plate for slicing and serving.

# Stuffed veal scallops

*These impressive veal parcels enclosing a meat, ham and mushroom filling are served here with
a hearty tomato sauce flavored with Armagnac, a French brandy from Gascony.*

*Preparation time 1 hour*
*Total cooking time 1 hour 15 minutes*
*Serves 4*

**8 small veal scallops, about 2 oz. each**
**16 slices lean bacon**
**all-purpose flour, for dusting**

**FILLING**
**4 oz. ground lean veal**
**3 oz. ground lean pork**
**1 1/2 tablespoons unsalted butter**
**2 shallots, finely chopped**
**1 cup mushrooms, chopped**
**1 oz. ham, chopped**
**1 tablespoon heavy cream**
**1 1/2 tablespoons fresh bread crumbs**
**2 tablespoons Armagnac or brandy**

**ARMAGNAC SAUCE**
**2 tablespoons unsalted butter**
**1 small carrot, chopped**
**1 small onion, chopped**
**1 stalk celery, chopped**
**3 tablespoons Armagnac or brandy**
**1 tablespoon tomato paste**
**1/3 cup all-purpose flour**
**2 cups chicken or brown stock (see**
  **pages 62 and 63)**
**3 tomatoes, peeled, seeded and chopped**
**bouquet garni (see page 63)**
**2 cloves garlic, chopped**

**1**  Preheat the oven to 400°F. Trim the veal of fat and
sinew, reserving the trimmings. Place the veal between
two sheets of plastic wrap and then flatten with a
meat mallet.

**2**  To make the filling, mix the ground meats in a bowl.
Melt the butter in a skillet. Add the shallots, then the
mushrooms, and cook over medium heat for
2–3 minutes, or until dry. Add the ham and cook for
2 minutes. Add the cream and simmer for 5 minutes, or
until thick. Remove from the heat and leave to cool,
then mix into the meat. Stir in the bread crumbs and
Armagnac and season to taste.

**3**  Spread a thin layer of filling onto the veal, then roll
up into neat parcels. Wrap a bacon strip or two around
each one, then tie up with kitchen string like a package.

**4**  To make the Armagnac sauce, melt the butter in a
large flameproof casserole or Dutch oven over medium
heat. Add the chopped carrot, onion, celery and veal
trimmings, and cook, without coloring, until the
onions are translucent. Add the Armagnac, cook for
2 minutes, then add the tomato paste and cook for
1–2 minutes. Sprinkle with the flour and cook for
2 minutes more. Stir in the stock, tomatoes, bouquet
garni and garlic. Season to taste with salt and pepper and
simmer for 10 minutes, skimming if necessary.

**5**  Melt some butter and oil in a skillet over medium
heat. Lightly dust the veal scallops with flour, then
brown them in the hot pan for 1–2 minutes. Add them
to the sauce, transfer to the oven and cook, uncovered,
for 25–30 minutes, basting once or twice.

**6**  Transfer the scallops to a dish; set aside and keep
warm. Strain the sauce into a clean saucepan and cook
for 10 minutes, skimming constantly. Remove and
discard the string and bacon from the scallops and
simmer in the sauce for 1–2 minutes. Slice and serve on
individual plates with the sauce poured over,
surrounded by vegetables such as glazed carrots, and
onions sprinkled with chopped fresh parsley.

# Lamb stew with potatoes

*This homely stew is perfect fare to combat the chill of winter evenings.*

*Preparation time **45 minutes***
*Total cooking time **2 hours***
*Serves 4*

2 lb. boneless lamb shoulder
3 tablespoons oil
3 tablespoons unsalted butter
1 large onion, finely chopped
1/4 cup tomato paste
1 tablespoon all-purpose flour
2 large tomatoes, peeled, seeded and chopped
3 cloves garlic, chopped
6 cups chicken stock (see page 62)
bouquet garni (see page 63)
12 small potatoes
1/4 cup chopped fresh parsley

**1** Preheat the oven to 400°F. Trim the lamb of fat and sinew and cut the meat into 1-inch cubes. Heat the oil in a heavy-bottomed skillet, then brown the lamb over medium-high heat. Drain, cover and set aside.

**2** In a flameproof casserole or Dutch oven, melt the butter and cook the onion over medium heat for 5 minutes, then add the tomato paste and cook for 2 minutes. Stir in the flour and cook for 2 minutes more. Add the tomatoes and cook for 3 minutes, then add the garlic and mix well. Add the lamb and any juices.

**3** In a saucepan, bring the stock to a boil, then add to the casserole and simmer for 1–2 minutes, skimming the foam. Add the bouquet garni and season to taste. Bake, covered, for 30 minutes. Uncover and bake for 30 minutes more.

**4** Add the potatoes. Bake for another 20–30 minutes, or until the potatoes are tender. Remove the bouquet garni and stir in the parsley just before serving.

# Molasses and almond tart

*Served warm with some whipped cream or a little freshly made vanilla custard, this deliciously sweet tart will enrich any winter's meal.*

*Preparation time 30 minutes + 20 minutes refrigeration*
*Total cooking time 35 minutes*
*Serves 8*

**PASTRY**
*1²/₃ cups all-purpose flour*
*large pinch of sugar*
*¹/₃ cup unsalted butter, chilled and cut into cubes*
*1 egg, lightly beaten*
*drop of vanilla extract*

**FILLING**
*¹/₃ cup unsalted butter, melted*
*juice and finely grated rind of 1 lemon*
*¹/₃ cup dark corn syrup*
*¹/₃ cup light molasses*
*1 cup ground almonds*
*1¹/₄ cups fresh bread crumbs*
*1 egg, beaten*
*²/₃ cup sliced almonds, to decorate*

**1** Brush a 9-inch fluted tart pan with removable base with melted butter. To make the pastry, sift the flour, sugar and a large pinch of salt into a large bowl. Rub the cubes of cold butter into the flour with a fast flicking action of the thumbs across the fingertips, until the mixture resembles fine bread crumbs.
**2** Make a well in the center and pour in the beaten egg, a teaspoon of water and a drop of vanilla. Slowly mix the pastry together by hand, or stir with a round-bladed knife into a rough ball. If the pastry is slightly sticky, add a little more flour. Turn out onto a cool, lightly floured surface, and knead very gently for no more than 20 seconds so that the pastry is just smooth. Cover with plastic wrap and refrigerate for at least 20 minutes before using. Preheat the oven to 400°F.
**3** Roll the pastry on a floured surface to about ¹/₈ inch thick. Line the tart pan with the pastry, pushing the pastry into the flutes of the pan with the help of a small ball of excess pastry. Trim off the excess pastry using a sharp knife, or roll a rolling pin across the top of the pan. Cut a circle of waxed paper 1¹/₄ inches larger than the tart pan, crush it into a ball, open it up and place it inside the pastry so that the liner comes up the sides.
**4** Fill the pan right up to the rim with rice or pie weights, then press down gently so they rest firmly against the sides of the pan. Transfer to the oven and bake for 12–15 minutes. Remove the rice or pie weights and discard the liner. If the pastry base looks wet, return the tart to the oven for 3–4 minutes. When cooked, remove from the oven and cool in the pan. Reduce the oven temperature to 350°F.
**5** To make the filling, combine all the filling ingredients except the sliced almonds in a large bowl. Stir briskly until smooth. Spread into the pastry shell and sprinkle with the sliced almonds. Bake for 15 minutes, or until the mixture feels set to the light touch of a finger. Remove from the oven, leave in the tart pan and place on a wire rack to cool before serving.

*Chef's tip* For a lighter flavor, leave out the molasses and use another ¹/₃ cup of dark corn syrup instead.

# Warm rhubarb and ginger cake with caramel sauce

*The sweetness of brown sugar and molasses in this comforting winter dessert is perfectly balanced by the tartness of rhubarb. The quantities of candied ginger can be adjusted to taste.*

Preparation time **20 minutes**
Total cooking time **1 hour**
**Serves 8**

**4 eggs**
**1/2 cup dark brown sugar**
**I teaspoon light molasses**
**3/4 cup all-purpose flour**
**I teaspoon finely chopped preserved or**
**    crystallized ginger**
**2 1/2 cups rhubarb, trimmed and diced**

**CARAMEL SAUCE**
**3/4 cup heavy cream**
**3/4 cup dark brown sugar**
**3 tablespoons unsalted butter**
**I teaspoon light molasses (optional)**
**I piece of preserved or crystallized ginger,**
**    chopped (optional)**

1 Preheat the oven to 325°F. Grease an 8-inch springform pan and line the base with a circle of waxed paper. Half-fill a medium saucepan with water, bring to a boil, then remove the pan from the heat.

2 Break the eggs into a heatproof bowl, add the brown sugar and place over the steaming pan of water, making sure the bowl does not touch the water. Beat with an electric mixer until the mixture is thick and mousse-like, then remove the bowl from the water and continue beating until cold. Beat in the molasses until well blended. Sift the flour and gently fold into the mixture, making sure all the flour is well incorporated to prevent lumps forming. Add the ginger.

3 Sprinkle half the diced rhubarb into the cake pan and cover with the cake mixture. Sprinkle the remaining rhubarb over the top. Bake for 35–40 minutes, or until the cake is firm to the touch and a skewer inserted into the center comes out clean.

4 To make the caramel sauce, warm the cream in a small saucepan over low heat to prevent the caramel forming lumps when the cream is added. Place the brown sugar in a separate pan over high heat, stirring constantly. As the sugar starts to melt, remove the pan from the heat and slowly stir in the cream to warm through. Whisk in the butter, then add the molasses and ginger if desired. Keep warm.

5 Turn the cake out onto a plate; remove the pan base and paper and serve with the sauce drizzled around, with a scoop of vanilla ice cream if desired.

***Chef's tip*** This dessert can be frozen.

# Fruit tarts with vanilla syrup

*The autumnal colors of dried fruit turn these melt-in-the-mouth shortbread treats—known to the French as* sablés aux fruits secs—*into an eye-catching delight.*

*Preparation time **20 minutes + 30 minutes resting***
*Total cooking time **20 minutes***
***Serves 4***

**SHORTBREAD PASTRY**
**2 cups all-purpose flour**
**1/2 cup confectioners' sugar**
**I teaspoon vanilla sugar (see Chef's tip)**
**2/3 cup unsalted butter, chilled and**
   **cut into cubes**

**FRUIT TOPPING**
**1 1/4 cups sugar**
**I vanilla bean, split in half**
**8 prunes, pitted**
**8 dried apricots**
**8 dates, pitted**
**I tablespoon dried currants**
**I carrot, very thinly sliced**
**I tablespoon chopped pistachios**
**I tablespoon sesame seeds**
**I tablespoon slivered almonds**

**1** Preheat the oven to 350°F. To make the pastry, sift the dry ingredients and some salt onto a work surface.

Make a well in the center, add the butter and mix it in with the fingertips until a dough forms that can be shaped into a ball. Flatten gently, place between two sheets of waxed paper, and roll out to a 1/4-inch thickness. Transfer to a baking sheet and chill for at least 20 minutes.

**2** To make the fruit topping, place the sugar, vanilla bean and 1 cup water in a saucepan and bring to a boil. Remove from the heat and add the prunes, apricots, dates, currants and carrot. Cover and leave to soak for 10 minutes. Remove the vanilla bean. Reserving the liquid, thoroughly drain the fruit and set aside. Bring the liquid to a boil and cook over high heat for 5–10 minutes, or until reduced to a syrup.

**3** Remove the top sheet of paper from the pastry and using a fluted cutter, cut four rounds 4 inches in diameter, placing them on a greased baking sheet. Bake for 10 minutes, or until just golden.

**4** Arrange the fruit on the four shortbread rounds. Sprinkle with the pistachios, sesame seeds and slivered almonds, and drizzle the syrup onto the serving plate around each shortbread. Serve with mascarpone cheese or heavy cream.

*Chef's tip* To make vanilla sugar, simply keep a vanilla bean in a jar of sugar.

# Steamed orange pudding

*Hot, light and full of flavor, this pudding will brighten the gloom of a winter's day like
a burst of summer sunshine. Serve with orange sauce or custard.*

Preparation time **30 minutes**
Total cooking time **1 hour 45 minutes**
**Serves 6**

1/3 cup thin-cut marmalade
2 large oranges, rind and pith removed
1/3 cup unsalted butter, at room temperature
1/2 cup sugar
finely grated rind of 1 orange
2 large eggs, beaten
1 1/2 cups self-rising flour
milk, for mixing

**ORANGE SAUCE**
1 1/4 cups orange juice
2 egg yolks
1/2 teaspoon cornstarch
3 tablespoons sugar
1 teaspoon Grand Marnier
    or Cointreau

**1**   Butter a 5-cup pudding mold measuring 6 inches across
the top. Cut two 11-inch circles, one from waxed paper,
one from foil. Place the paper on the foil, then brush the
paper with softened butter. Fold the paper and foil to
make a 3/4-inch pleat in the center, to allow the pudding
to expand.

**2**   Spoon the marmalade into the pudding mold. Thinly
slice the oranges, then line the mold with the orange
slices, from the marmalade base to the top of the bowl.

**3**   In a bowl, beat the butter with a wooden spoon or
electric mixer to soften. Slowly add the sugar, beating
until light and fluffy. Mix in the orange rind. Add the
eggs in four additions, beating well after each addition.

Sift in the flour and quickly fold into the mixture using
a large metal spoon or plastic spatula. As the last traces
of flour are mixed in, add a little milk to make a soft
consistency: the mixture should drop from the spoon
with a flick of the wrist.

**4**   Immediately transfer the mixture to the pudding
mold. Cover with the circle of paper and foil, placing
the sheet foil-side-up, and tie with kitchen string to seal.
Place a saucer or trivet in a large saucepan and rest
the pudding mold on it. Half-fill the pan with boiling
water and bring to a boil. Making sure the water
is gently bubbling at all times, and adding more boiling
water as necessary, steam the pudding, covered, for
1 1/2–1 3/4 hours, or until springy to the light touch of
a finger.

**5**   When cooked, carefully remove the pudding from
the steamer. Remove the foil and paper, place a warm
plate over the pudding mold and carefully turn the
pudding over and remove the bowl. (If you are not
serving the pudding immediately, place the bowl back
over the pudding to prevent it from drying out.)

**6**   To make the orange sauce, bring the orange juice to a
boil in a small saucepan. In a bowl, beat the egg yolks,
cornstarch and sugar until thick and light. Pour the hot
orange juice into the bowl, mix until blended, then
return to the pan. Cook over medium heat, stirring
constantly with a wooden spoon, until the mixture coats
the back of the spoon and the sauce does not close over
when a line is drawn across the spoon with a finger.

**7**   Remove from the heat, strain into a bowl, then stir in
the Grand Marnier or Cointreau. If you are not using
the sauce right away, dust the surface lightly with sugar
to prevent a skin forming. The sugar can be stirred in
just before serving. Serve the sauce warm or cold with
the pudding.

# Chocolate and chestnut terrine

*This rich, chilled terrine is a terrific dessert for unexpected guests. It freezes well for up to 3 months. Serve thinly sliced.*

*Preparation time* **20 minutes + 12 hours refrigeration**
*Total cooking time* **10 minutes**
***Serves 10–12***

**6 oz. good-quality semisweet chocolate, chopped**
**¹/3 cup unsalted butter, at room temperature**
**¹/3 cup sugar**
**12 oz. canned unsweetened chestnut purée**
**¹/4 teaspoon vanilla extract**
**¹/4 teaspoon instant coffee, dissolved in I teaspoon hot water**
**2 tablespoons rum**
**good-quality semisweet chocolate, for shaving**
**fresh berries or orange segments, to garnish**

1   Grease an 8¹/2 x 4¹/2 x 2¹/2-inch loaf pan or ceramic terrine. Line the base with waxed paper, then oil the paper.

2   Place the chocolate in the top of a double boiler over hot water and stir until melted. Remove the insert from the water and leave to cool for 5 minutes.

3   In a mixing bowl, beat the butter to soften, then add the sugar and beat until pale and light. Beat in the chestnut purée until softened, then the melted chocolate until thoroughly blended. Mix in the vanilla, coffee and rum. Transfer the mixture to the prepared loaf pan, smooth the top, cover with plastic wrap or foil, and refrigerate for 12 hours.

4   To serve, loosen the sides of the terrine using a small palette or round-bladed knife; turn out the terrine and remove the paper. Using a vegetable peeler, shave off curls from the edge of the chocolate bar and use these to garnish the terrine. Slice and serve with fresh berries or orange segments.

# Pears poached in red wine

*A light yet satisfying end to a meal, this colorful dessert can be dressed up even further
by adding some prunes to poach with the pears in the spiced wine syrup.*

*Preparation time **25 minutes***
*Total cooking time **50 minutes***
***Serves 4***

**6 cups full-bodied red wine**
  **(such as Cabernet Sauvignon)**
**1³/4 cups sugar**
**2 cinnamon sticks**
**1 vanilla bean**
**1 whole clove**
**rind of 1 lemon**
**rind of 1 orange**
**4 pears**
**3 tablespoons red currant jelly**
**2 oranges**
**fresh mint leaves, to garnish**
**fresh raspberries or red currants, to garnish**

1  In a heavy-bottomed saucepan, bring the wine,
1¹/4 cups of the sugar, the spices, lemon rind and orange
rind to a boil.
2  Peel the pears, leaving the stems intact, and remove
the blossom end using the tip of a vegetable peeler or a
small knife. Place the pears in the hot wine, cover with
a round of aluminum foil or waxed paper, and simmer
over low heat for about 20 minutes, or until tender to
the point of a sharp knife, turning or basting the pears if
the liquid does not cover them completely. (The actual
cooking time will depend on their ripeness.) Remove
the pears from the wine and set aside to cool.
3  Bring the wine to a boil, then reduce the heat and
simmer for 15 minutes, or until reduced in volume by
one third. Add the red currant jelly and allow it to melt
completely, then strain and set aside to cool.
4  Thinly peel the oranges using a vegetable peeler,
avoiding the bitter white pith. Cut the rind into very
thin strips and place in a small saucepan with cold
water. Bring to a boil, then drain and rinse well in cold
water. Drain the rind and set aside. In the same pan, mix
the remaining sugar with 1 cup water and boil until the
sugar dissolves. Add the drained rind, reduce the
heat and simmer for 2–3 minutes, or until the syrup
thickens and the rind has absorbed the sugar and
appears translucent.
5  Carefully arrange the pears in a serving dish and
cover with the wine syrup. Sprinkle with the orange
rind, garnish with mint and decorate with raspberries or
red currants.

***Chef's tip*** For a rich, dark color, soak the pears in the
poaching liquid overnight.

# Baked rice pudding

*This classic favorite, so simple to prepare, cooks gently in a slow oven, allowing the rice to absorb all the liquid. The result is delightfully soft and creamy.*

*Preparation time 5 minutes + 30 minutes standing*
*Total cooking time 2 hours*
*Serves 4*

*3 cups milk*
*1 1/2 tablespoons sugar*
*2–3 drops vanilla extract*
*1/3 cup short-grain rice*
*1 teaspoon unsalted butter*
*freshly grated nutmeg, to taste*

**1**  Combine the milk, sugar, vanilla and rice in a 3-cup baking dish, and leave to stand for 30 minutes. Preheat the oven to 350°F.
**2**  Dot the butter over the mixture, sprinkle some grated nutmeg over the top and cover with a lid or aluminum foil. Place the dish on the middle shelf of the oven and bake for 1 hour, stirring once or twice with a fork.
**3**  Remove the lid and reduce the oven temperature to 300°F. If serving the pudding cold, bake for another 45 minutes, remove from the oven, leave to cool, then refrigerate. If serving the pudding hot, cook for a full hour, or until a brown skin forms and the interior of the pudding is soft and creamy. Serve hot with a teaspoon of good strawberry jam, or cold with your choice of fresh red berries or poached red fruit such as plums.

***Chef's tips*** If the rice pudding is too dry, adjust the consistency before serving by simply lifting the skin to one side and adding a little cold milk.

To vary the flavor, use cinnamon in place of the vanilla and nutmeg, or sprinkle 1–2 tablespoons golden raisins or chopped mixed candied citrus peel or citron in with the rice before cooking.

# Mincemeat tart

*This mincemeat tart is made luxurious by the addition of fresh fruit, and is elegant and delicious*
*served warm with whipped cream melting onto the fruit through the opening in the pastry.*

Preparation time **30 minutes + 50 minutes refrigeration**
Total cooking time **45 minutes**
**Serves 6–8**

**FRUIT FILLING**
I small Granny Smith apple, peeled and diced
I small ripe pear, peeled and diced
2 tablespoons mixed candied citrus peel or citron
I cup dark raisins
I cup dried currants
I cup golden raisins
3/4 cup fresh black grapes, seeded
1/4 cup halved or slivered almonds
1/4 cup coarsely chopped walnuts
pinch of nutmeg
pinch of cinnamon
1/2 cup soft brown sugar
grated rind and juice of 1/2 orange
grated rind of 1/2 lemon
2 tablespoons brandy
I tablespoon unsalted butter, melted

**SHORT PASTRY**
2 1/2 cups all-purpose flour
2/3 cup unsalted butter, chilled and cut into cubes
I egg, lightly beaten
I–2 drops vanilla extract

I egg white
sugar, to garnish
I cup whipping cream

1   Preheat the oven to 425°F. Brush a 9 x 1 1/4-inch flan ring with melted butter and place on a baking sheet.
2   To make the fruit filling, place the filling ingredients in a large bowl. Mix thoroughly and set aside.

3   To make the pastry, sift the flour with a large pinch of salt into a large bowl. Rub the cubes of butter into the flour with your fingertips until the mixture resembles fine bread crumbs. Make a well in the center and pour in the egg, vanilla and 2 teaspoons water. Slowly mix together to a rough ball. If it is slightly sticky, add a little extra flour. Turn onto a lightly floured surface and knead very gently for no more than 20 seconds, or until just smooth. Cover with plastic wrap and chill for at least 20 minutes before using.
4   On a floured surface, roll out two thirds of the pastry to a circle 3/4 inch wider than the flan ring. Line the ring with pastry, pressing gently against the sides, then roll a rolling pin across the top to remove the excess. Thoroughly drain the fruit filling in a colander, then fill the pastry shell using a slotted spoon.
5   Roll the remaining pastry to a 9-inch circle, to fit just inside the flan ring. Using a 3 1/2-inch round cutter, cut a round from the center of the pastry and discard. Place the pastry over the mincemeat filling, pinch the edges to seal, then trim the edges of excess pastry and refrigerate for 30 minutes.
6   Transfer to the oven and bake for 30–35 minutes. Whisk the egg white until stiff, remove the tart from the oven and brush the pastry with the egg. Sprinkle well with sugar and bake for 10 minutes more, or until golden brown and "frosty."
7   Transfer to a plate and discard the flan ring. Beat the cream until it holds its shape and spoon some onto the hole in the center of the tart. Serve the tart warm and offer the remaining cream separately.

*Chef's tips* Be sure to drain the fruit filling thoroughly in step 4, so the tart does not become soggy.
   You can buy flan rings from cookware stores.

# Apple fritters

*For a simple family supper, apple slices, tossed in Calvados and sugar and coated in a light, golden batter, are always a welcome treat.*

*Preparation time* **35 minutes**
*Total cooking time* **20 minutes**
*Serves 6–8*

**5–6 Golden Delicious apples, peeled and cored**
**1/2 cup sugar**
**1/3 cup Calvados or applejack**
**2 1/3 cups all-purpose flour**
**2 1/2 tablespoons cornstarch**
**2 eggs**
**1 cup beer**
**1 tablespoon oil**
**oil, for deep-frying**
**4 egg whites**
**confectioners' sugar, to dust**

1   Slice the apples into 1/2-inch rounds so that each has a hole in the center. Combine 1/3 cup of the sugar with the Calvados in a small bowl. Coat the apples in the mixture and set aside.
2   Sift the flour, cornstarch and some salt into a large bowl. Make a well in the center, add the eggs and begin to whisk in the flour, then gradually whisk in the beer until all the flour is incorporated and the batter is smooth and lump-free. Stir in the oil and set aside.
3   Heat a deep-fat fryer or deep saucepan, one-third full of oil, to 325°F. Beat the egg whites into soft peaks, then add the remaining sugar and beat until smooth and glossy. Fold the mixture into the batter using a large metal spoon. (The mixture will be very thick.)
4   Drain the apples well and dry with paper towels. Dip single slices into the batter and place in the hot oil in batches to brown, turning to brown both sides. Drain on paper towels, sprinkle with confectioners' sugar and serve hot.

# Apple meringues with raspberry coulis

*The crisp crown of meringue in this golden dessert harbors a smooth, marshmallowy interior. For special occasions, flambé the apples with brandy or rum instead of—or as well as—the raspberry sauce.*

*Preparation time **45 minutes***
*Total cooking time **40 minutes***
***Serves 4***

**1 cup sugar**
**grated rind of 1/4 lemon**
**1/2 vanilla bean, split**
**4 large apples**
**1 tablespoon unsalted butter**
**1 tablespoon chopped golden raisins**
**1 tablespoon chopped mixed candied citrus peel**
**or citron**
**1 tablespoon chopped pitted dates, dried prunes**
**or apricots**
**2 egg whites**
**2 cups fresh raspberries**
**1/4 cup confectioners' sugar, and extra**
**for dusting**
**lemon juice, to taste**

1  Place 2/3 cup of the sugar, the lemon rind and vanilla bean in a saucepan with 1 1/4 cups water. Stir over gentle heat to dissolve the sugar. Bring to a boil, then reduce the heat to a simmer.

2  Peel and core the apples, then add them to the pan and baste well in the simmering syrup. Cover and poach gently for 10 minutes, or until just tender, basting occasionally. Remove the apples and leave to cool. Set the syrup aside.

3  Melt the butter in a small skillet; add the chopped fruit and enough of the syrup to moisten. Cook over low heat for 4 minutes. Spoon the mixture into the apples and place them well apart on a lightly greased baking sheet. Preheat the oven to 325°F.

4  To make the meringue, beat the egg whites into stiff peaks in a deep bowl. Add 3 tablespoons of the sugar, 2 teaspoons at a time, beating well after each addition to form a satin-smooth mixture. In one addition, gently fold in the remaining sugar until just blended.

5  Using a pastry bag fitted with a 1/2-inch star nozzle, pipe a spiral of the mixture around each apple, from base to top, leaving a hole in the top. Alternatively, spoon on the mixture and lift it into spiky peaks using a tablespoon. Dust with confectioners' sugar and bake for 20 minutes, or until a pale, golden brown.

6  To make the coulis, purée the raspberries in a blender with the confectioners' sugar. Pass through a fine sieve to remove the seeds, and add lemon juice to taste. Serve the apple meringues hot or warm on individual plates, with the raspberry coulis poured around the base and dusted with the extra confectioners' sugar.

# Chef's techniques

◆

## Shaping quenelles

*These oval-shaped dumplings can be used as a main meal or to garnish clear soups.*

Test the quenelle mixture for seasoning by cooking a teaspoonful of the mixture in the barely simmering stock or water.

Drain and cut through with a knife to check if it is cooked. Taste for seasoning.

Shape the quenelles by scooping up some mousse with a spoon and transferring it to a second spoon, then scooping back and forth between the two spoons until the quenelle is smooth and oval with three edges.

Once shaped, wet the empty spoon and use it to scoop the quenelle off the other spoon into the barely simmering liquid. Repeat with the remaining mousse mixture.

## Making chicken stock

*Good, flavorful homemade stock can be the cornerstone of a great dish.*

Cut up 1 1/2 lb. chicken bones and carcass and put in a pan with a coarsely chopped onion, carrot and celery stalk. Add 6 peppercorns, a bouquet garni and 4 quarts water.

Bring to a boil and let the stock simmer gently for 2–3 hours, skimming off any foam that rises to the surface using a large spoon. Strain the stock through a sieve into a clean bowl, then allow to cool.

Chill the stock overnight, then lift off any fat. If you can't leave overnight, skim, then drag the surface of the hot strained stock with paper towels to lift off the fat. Makes 6–8 cups.

# Making brown stock

*Roasting the bones gives a good color to the stock and helps to remove the excess fat.*

In a 450°F oven, roast 3 lb. beef or veal bones for 40 minutes, adding a quartered onion, 2 chopped carrots, 1 chopped leek and 1 chopped celery stalk halfway through.

Transfer to a clean saucepan. Add 4 quarts water, 2 tablespoons tomato paste, bouquet garni and 6 peppercorns. Simmer for 3–4 hours, skimming often.

Ladle the stock in batches into a fine sieve over a bowl. Gently press the solids with the ladle to extract all the liquid and place in the refrigerator to cool. Lift off any fat. Makes 6–8 cups.

# Freezing stock

*Stock will keep in the refrigerator for 3 days. It can be frozen in portions for later use, for 6 months.*

After removing any fat, boil the stock until reduced to 2 cups. Cool and freeze until solid. Transfer to a plastic freezer bag and seal. To make 2 quarts stock, add 6 cups water to 2 cups concentrated stock.

# Carving a duck

*Unlike chickens, ducks have little leg meat. Carving makes sure everyone gets a portion of breast meat.*

Place the duck breast-side-up on a chopping board. Steadying the duck with a carving fork, cut the legs from the bird with a large carving knife.

At each shoulder joint, cut the wings away from the body of the duck.

Moving towards the breast bone, cut the breast meat into slices. Repeat on the other side.

# Bouquet garni

*Add the flavor and aroma of herbs to your dish with a freshly made bouquet garni.*

Wrap the green part of a leek loosely around a bay leaf, a sprig of thyme, some celery leaves and a few stalks of parsley, then tie with string. Leave a long tail to the string for easy removal.

First published in the United States in 1998 by Periplus Editions (HK) Ltd., with editorial offices at
153 Milk Street, Boston, Massachusetts 02109.

Murdoch Books and Le Cordon Bleu thank the 32 masterchefs of all the Le Cordon Bleu Schools, whose knowledge and
expertise have made this book possible, especially: Chef Cliche (MOF), Chef Terrien, Chef Boucheret, Chef Duchêne (MOF),
Chef Guillut, Chef Steneck, Paris; Chef Males, Chef Walsh, Chef Hardy, London; Chef Chantefort, Chef Bertin, Chef Jambert,
Chef Honda, Tokyo; Chef Salembien, Chef Boutin, Chef Harris, Sydney; Chef Lawes, Adelaide; Chef Guiet, Chef Denis, Ottawa.
Of the many students who helped the Chefs test each recipe, a special mention to graduates David Welch and Allen Wertheim.
A very special acknowledgment to Directors Susan Eckstein, Great Britain, and Kathy Shaw, Paris, who have been responsible for
the coordination of the Le Cordon Bleu team throughout this series.

The Publisher and Le Cordon Bleu wish to thank Carole Sweetnam for her help with this series.

First published in Australia in 1998 by Murdoch Books®

Managing Editor: Kay Halsey
Series Concept, Design and Art Direction: Juliet Cohen
Editor: Katri Hilden
Food Director: Jody Vassallo
Food Editors: Lulu Grimes, Tracy Rutherford
US Editor: Linda Venturoni Wilson
Designer: Wing Ping Tong
Photographers: Jon Bader, Joe Filshie
Food Stylists: Amanda Cooper, Carolyn Fienberg
Food Preparation: Christine Sheppard, Jo Forrest, Kerrie Ray
Chef's Techniques Photographer: Reg Morrison
Home Economists: Anna Last, Michelle Lawton, Toiva Longhurst, Kerrie Mullins, Angela Nahas, Kerrie Ray

Library of Congress catalog card number: 98-65974
ISBN 962-593-437-5

Front cover: Beef Wellington

Distributed in the United States by
Charles E. Tuttle Co., Inc.
RR1 Box 231-5
North Clarendon, VT 05759
Tel: (802) 773-8930
Fax: (802) 773-6993

Printed in Singapore

05 04 03 02 01 00 99 98  10 9 8 7 6 5 4 3 2 1

Important: Some of the recipes in this book may include raw eggs, which can cause salmonella poisoning.
Those who might be at risk from this (the elderly, pregnant women, young children and those suffering
from immune deficiency diseases) should check with their physicians before eating raw eggs.